MOOKIE BETTS

SPORTS SUPERSTARS

BY THOMAS K. ADAMSON

BELLWETHER MEDIA • MINNEAPOLIS, MN

Torque brims with excitement perfect for thrill-seekers of all kinds. Discover daring survival skills, explore uncharted worlds, and marvel at mighty engines and extreme sports. In *Torque* books, anything can happen. Are you ready?

This edition first published in 2025 by Bellwether Media, Inc.

No part of this publication may be reproduced in whole or in part without written permission of the publisher. For information regarding permission, write to Bellwether Media, Inc., Attention: Permissions Department, 6012 Blue Circle Drive, Minnetonka, MN 55343.

Library of Congress Cataloging-in-Publication Data

Names: Adamson, Thomas K., 1970- author.
Title: Mookie Betts / by Thomas K. Adamson.
Description: Minneapolis, MN : Bellwether Media, 2025. | Series: Torque. Sports superstars | Includes bibliographical references and index. | Audience: Ages 7-12 | Audience: Grades 4-6 | Summary: "Engaging images accompany information about Mookie Betts. The combination of high-interest subject matter and light text is intended for students in grades 3 through 7"– Provided by publisher.
Identifiers: LCCN 2024010423 (print) | LCCN 2024010424 (ebook) | ISBN 9798893040364 (library binding) | ISBN 9781644879740 (ebook)
Subjects: LCSH: Betts, Mookie, 1992–Juvenile literature. | Baseball players–United States–Biography–Juvenile literature.
Classification: LCC GV865.B488 A74 2025 (print) | LCC GV865.B488 (ebook) | DDC 796.357092 [B]–dc23/eng/20230314
LC record available at https://lccn.loc.gov/2024010423
LC ebook record available at https://lccn.loc.gov/2024010424

Text copyright © 2025 by Bellwether Media, Inc. TORQUE and associated logos are trademarks and/or registered trademarks of Bellwether Media, Inc. Bellwether Media is a division of Chrysalis Education Group.

Editor: Kieran Downs   Designer: Gabriel Hilger

Printed in the United States of America, North Mankato, MN.

TABLE OF CONTENTS

WORLD SERIES BLAST	4
WHO IS MOOKIE BETTS?	6
A GROWING TALENT	8
BASEBALL SUPERSTAR	12
BOWLING AND BASEBALL	20
GLOSSARY	22
TO LEARN MORE	23
INDEX	24

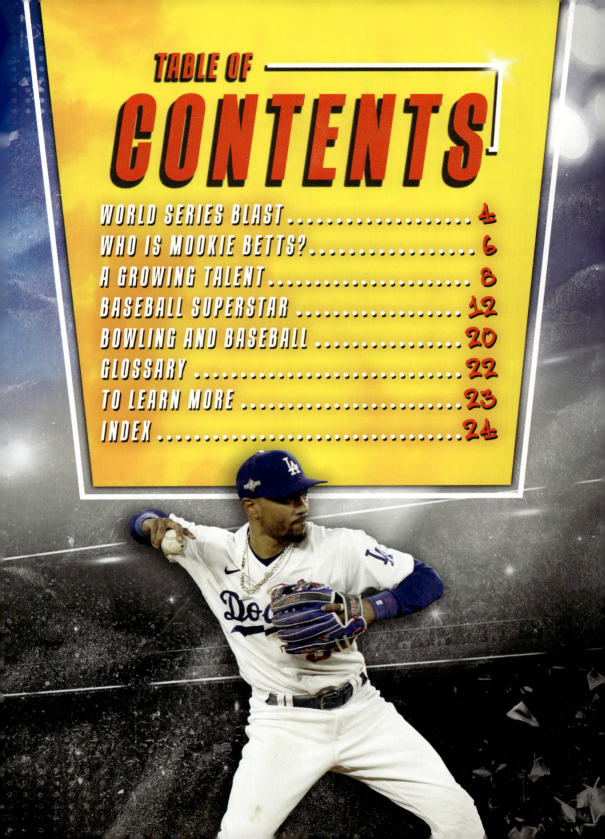

WORLD SERIES BLAST

It is Game 6 of the 2020 **World Series**. The Dodgers lead the Rays by one run. Mookie Betts leads off the bottom of the 8th inning.

With two strikes, Betts hits the ball over the fence for a **home run**! The added run helps the Dodgers win the game and their first World Series since 1988!

WHO IS MOOKIE BETTS?

Mookie Betts is an **outfielder** and **infielder** in **Major League Baseball** (MLB). He was named the **Most Valuable Player** (MVP) of the **American League** (AL) in 2018. He has won the World Series with two different teams.

Name Game

Betts's full name is Markus Lynn Betts. His parents are basketball fans. Betts's nickname comes from basketball player Mookie Blaylock.

MOOKIE BETTS

BIRTHDAY	October 7, 1992
HOMETOWN	Nashville, Tennessee
POSITION	outfielder, infielder
HEIGHT	5 feet 9 inches
DRAFTED	Drafted by the Boston Red Sox in the 5th round (172nd overall) of the 2011 MLB Draft

Betts is also a bowler! He bowls nearly every day in the offseason.

A GROWING TALENT

Betts has played baseball since he was a kid. At age 5, Betts tried to get on a Little League team. The coach thought he was too small. His mom formed a new team with kids like Betts.

BETTS WITH HIS MOM

TWO-SPORT TALENT

Betts learned bowling before baseball. His mom taught him to bowl at age 3.

In high school, Betts bowled and played baseball and basketball. In 2010, he played at a baseball showcase. A Boston Red Sox **scout** noticed him.

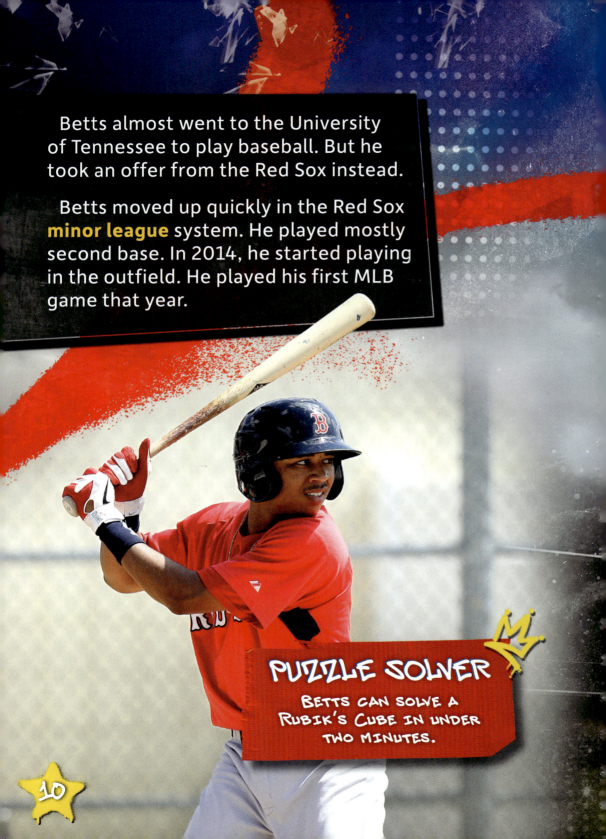

Betts almost went to the University of Tennessee to play baseball. But he took an offer from the Red Sox instead.

Betts moved up quickly in the Red Sox **minor league** system. He played mostly second base. In 2014, he started playing in the outfield. He played his first MLB game that year.

PUZZLE SOLVER

Betts can solve a Rubik's Cube in under two minutes.

FAVORITES

FOOD	MOVIE	TV SHOW	SPORT OTHER THAN BASEBALL
 strawberry shortcake	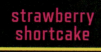 Life	POWER Power	bowling

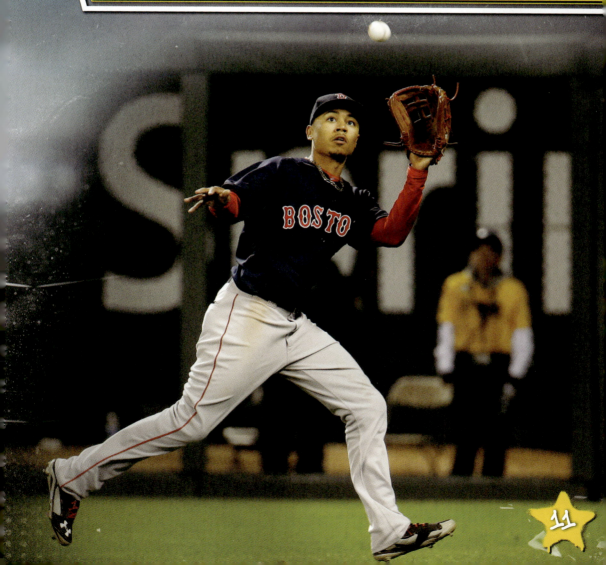

11

BASEBALL SUPERSTAR

Betts hit a home run in the first game of the 2015 season. He was a solid hitter all season.

Starting in 2016, Betts became a superstar. He played in his first **All-Star Game**. He helped the Red Sox win the **division**. He also won his first **Gold Glove** and **Silver Slugger** awards.

2016 ALL-STAR GAME

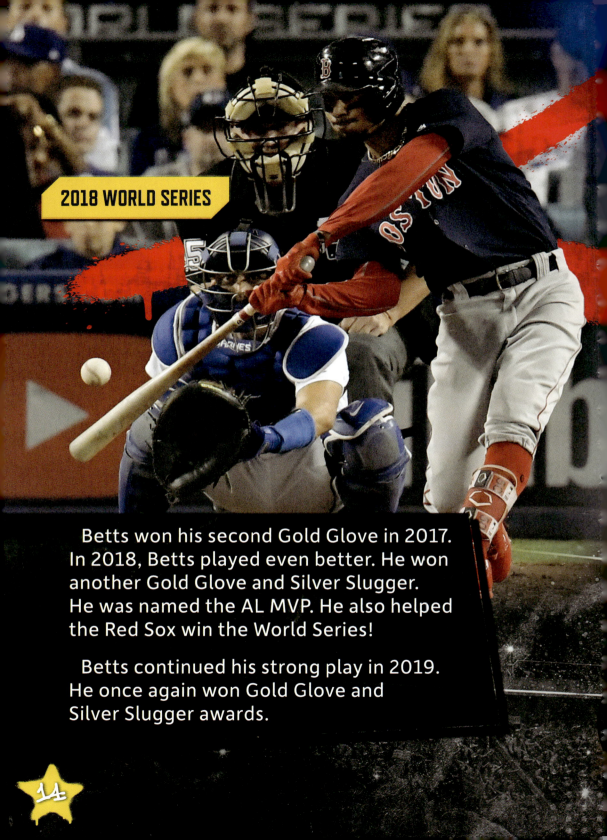

2018 WORLD SERIES

    Betts won his second Gold Glove in 2017. In 2018, Betts played even better. He won another Gold Glove and Silver Slugger. He was named the AL MVP. He also helped the Red Sox win the World Series!

    Betts continued his strong play in 2019. He once again won Gold Glove and Silver Slugger awards.

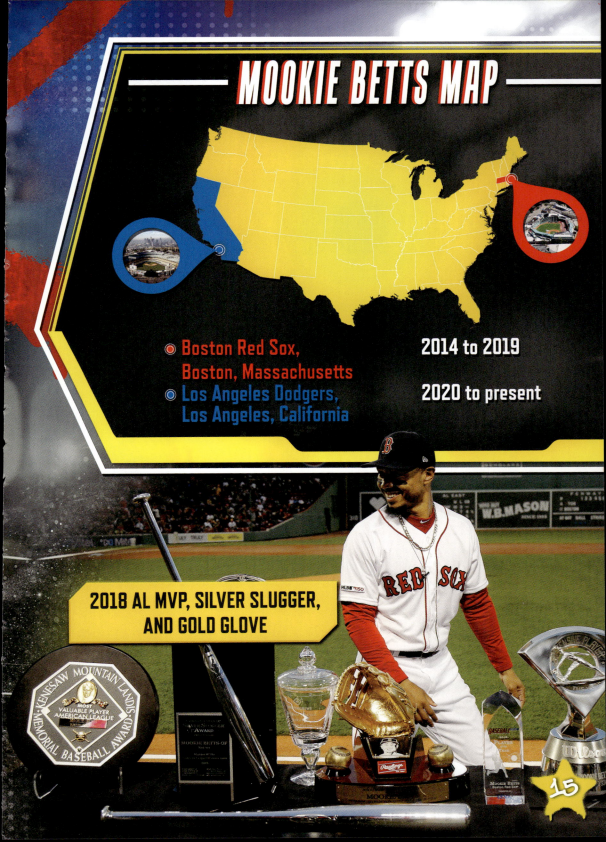

In 2020, the Red Sox traded Betts. He joined the Los Angeles Dodgers before the season started. Betts was a solid hitter in the shortened 2020 season. He helped the Dodgers win the World Series.

In 2021, he hurt his hip. But he still played well enough to be voted into the All-Star Game.

2020 WORLD SERIES

Betts came back strong in 2022. He won another Gold Glove and Silver Slugger. He also played in the All-Star Game.

In 2023, Betts hit 39 home runs. He returned to the All-Star Game. He won his sixth Silver Slugger. He also started playing a lot more games in the infield.

2022 ALL-STAR GAME

TIMELINE

— **2014** —
Betts plays in his first MLB game

— **October 2018** —
The Red Sox win the World Series

— **November 2018** —
Betts wins the AL MVP Award

18

POWER HITTING
Betts has hit three home runs in one game six different times. He is tied with two other players for this record.

— 2020 —
Betts is traded to the Dodgers

— 2020 —
The Dodgers win the World Series

— 2023 —
Betts wins his sixth Silver Slugger

19

BOWLING AND BASEBALL

Betts combines his love for bowling with his fame as a baseball star to help kids. He started a **foundation** to help kids in need. Through the 5050 Foundation, Betts has held bowling events to raise money.

Most of all, he wants to bring another World Series to Dodgers fans!

21

GLOSSARY

All-Star Game—a game between the best players in a league

American League—one of the two large groupings of teams in Major League Baseball; the other is the National League.

division—a group of teams from the same area that often play against each other

foundation—an organization that helps people and communities

Gold Glove—an award recognizing the best fielder of each position in MLB

home run—a hit where the batter runs all the way around the bases and scores a run

infielder—a position in baseball in which a player stands closer to the batter to field ground balls

Major League Baseball—a professional baseball league in the United States; Major League Baseball is often called MLB.

minor league—related to professional baseball leagues below Major League Baseball

most valuable player—the best player in a year, game, or series; the most valuable player is often called the MVP.

outfielder—a position in baseball in which a player stands far away from the batter to catch hit balls

scout—a person who watches players in action and recommends them for a team

Silver Slugger—an award recognizing the best hitter of each position in baseball

World Series—the championship series in Major League Baseball, played between the best team in the American League and the best team in the National League

TO LEARN MORE

AT THE LIBRARY

Abdo, Kenny. *Mookie Betts*. Minneapolis, Minn.: Abdo Zoom, 2021.

Chandler, Matt. *Mookie Betts: Baseball Champion.* North Mankato, Minn.: Capstone, 2023.

Peterson, Megan Cooley. *Los Angeles Dodgers*. Mankato, Minn.: Creative Education and Creative Paperbacks, 2024.

ON THE WEB

Factsurfer.com gives you a safe, fun way to find more information.

1. Go to www.factsurfer.com

2. Enter "Mookie Betts" into the search box and click 🔍.

3. Select your book cover to see a list of related content.

INDEX

5050 Foundation, 20
All-Star Game, 13, 16, 18
American League, 6, 14, 15
awards, 6, 13, 14, 15, 18
Boston Red Sox, 9, 10, 13, 14, 16
bowling, 7, 8, 9, 20
childhood, 8, 9
division, 13
family, 6, 8
favorites, 11
future, 21
Gold Glove, 13, 14, 15, 18
home run, 4, 12, 18, 19
hurt, 16
infielder, 6, 10, 18
Los Angeles Dodgers, 4, 16, 21
Major League Baseball, 6, 10
map, 15
minor league, 10
most valuable player, 6, 14, 15
name, 6
outfielder, 6, 10
profile, 7
record, 19
Rubik's Cube, 10
scout, 9
Silver Slugger, 13, 14, 15, 18
timeline, 18–19
trade, 16
trophy shelf, 17
University of Tennessee, 10
World Series, 4, 6, 14, 16, 21

The images in this book are reproduced through the courtesy of: Brian Rothmuller/ Icon Sportswire/ AP Images, front cover; Kevin Reece/ AP Images, p. 3; Cooper Neill/ Stringer/ Getty, p. 4; Sean M. Haffey/ Staff/ Getty, pp. 4-5; Ryan Sun/ AP Images, p. 6; Steve Cukrov, p. 7 (Dodgers logo); Connor P. Fitzgerald, p. 7 (Mookie Betts); Kevork Djansezian/ Contributor/ Getty, p. 8; Mat Hayward/ Stringer/ Getty, pp. 9, 20; Mike Janes/ AP Images, p. 10; vm2002, p. 11 (strawberry shortcake); Cinematic/ Alamy, p. 11 (*Life*); STARZ/ Wikipedia, p. 11 (*Power*); Andrey Burmakin, p. 11 (bowling); Charlie Riedel/ AP Images, p. 11 (Mookie Betts); Steve Senne/ AP Images, p. 12; Bill Nichols/ AP Images, p. 13; Mark J. Terril/ AP Images, p. 14; Richard Cavalleri, p. 15 (Red Sox Stadium); Emma_Griffiths, p. 15 (Dodgers Stadium); Winslow Townson/ AP Images, pp. 15 (2018 AL MVP, Silver Slugger, and Gold Glove), 19 (2018 AL MVP award); Sue Ogrocki/ AP Images, p. 16; Ashley Landis/ AP Images, p. 17; Pool/ AP Images, p. 18 (2022 All-Star Game); Jae C. Hong/ AP Images, pp. 18 (2018 World Series), 18-19; Los Angeles Dodgers/ Wikipedia, p. 19 (Dodgers logo); Kirby Lee/ Alamy, p. 21; Brian Rothmuller/ Icon Sportswire/ Ap Images, p. 23.